MW00979648

Order this book online at www.trafford.com
or email orders@trafford.com

Most Trafford titles are also available at major online book retailers.

© Copyright 2012 Kathy Johnson.
All rights reserved. No part of this publication may be reproduced, stored in a retrieval system, or
transmitted, in any form or by any means, electronic, mechanical, photocopying, recording, or
otherwise, without the written prior permission of the author.

Printed in the United States of America.

ISBN: 978-1-4669-3252-4

*Trafford rev. 5/21/2012*

 www.trafford.com

**North America & international**
toll-free: 1 888 232 4444 (USA & Canada)
phone: 250 383 6864 ♦ fax: 812 355 4082

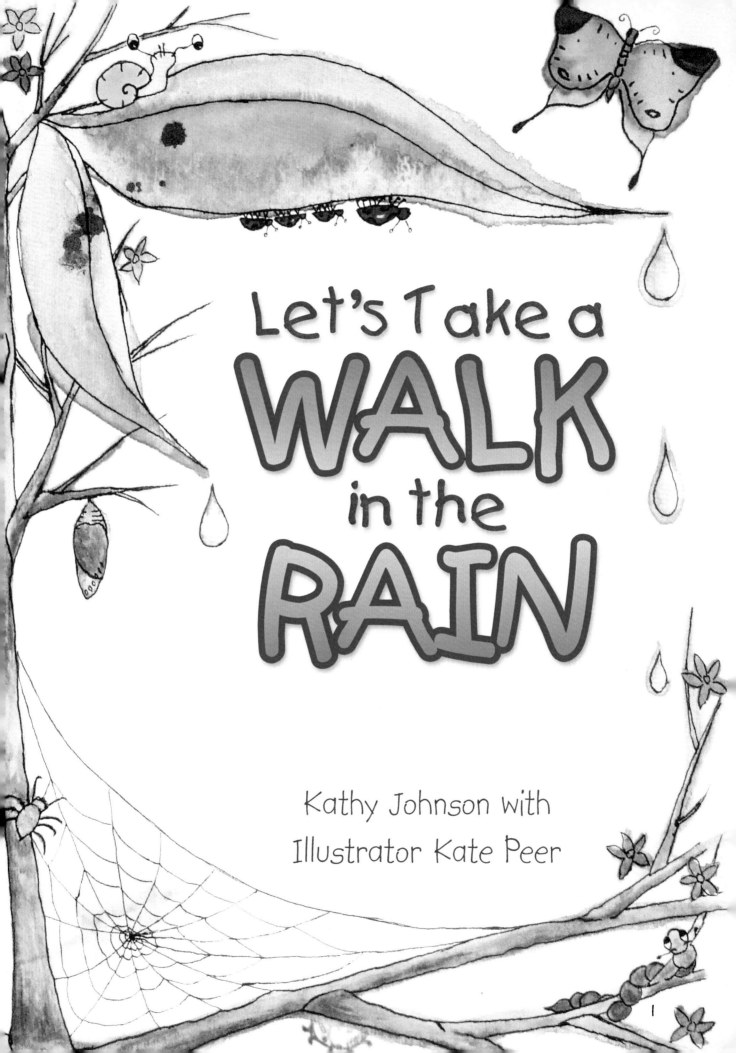

# Let's Take a
# WALK
# in the
# RAIN

Kathy Johnson with

Illustrator Kate Peer

# Dedication:

To all the children in our lives, present and future.

# Note to Parents

An appreciation of nature and gratitude for the world around us is one of the greatest gifts we can pass on to our children. Let's Take a Walk in the Rain is meant to be a guide for spending a part of the day together with your child. Enjoy the simple words and delightful illustrations in the book, take a relaxed walk outdoors making awareness and appreciation of your surroundings a focus, and finish off with a craft project that allows your child's imagination to soar.

It can be great fun to gather basic craft supplies while you walk. Simple treasures like rocks, leaves, branches and cones will excite and stimulate your child's creative mind. On the final pages you'll find ingredients for a simple craft box, along with a few ideas to help get started. The internet is also a wonderful resource for discovering new craft ideas.

There are endless opportunities for discovery and creative inspiration in the great outdoors: Wind is blowing, plants are growing, insects are humming, sun is nourishing, and sometimes nature is getting a drink of water!

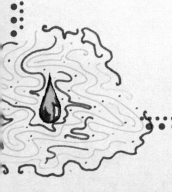

# Let's Take a Walk in the Rain.

Should we wear our boots and raincoats?

Maybe we'll find a
puddle to jump in!

Wouldn't it be fun to catch raindrops on our tongues?

# Let's listen for all the rainy day sounds.

# Look up:
# What shapes and colours has nature drawn in the clouds?

Take a deep breath:
Even the roads and
sidewalks smell
different in the rain.

Look how happy
nature is to be getting
a drink of water.

19

# Rain gives life to plants and animals and us!

# Craft Box Ingredients

- plastic table cloth for protecting tables or floors
- construction paper
- white paper
- white glue
- glue sticks
- craft glue gun for use by an adult
- glitter or glitter glue
- wax crayons
- non toxic felt pens
- pencils and pencil crayons
- pencil sharpener
- stapler
- safety scissors
- paint brushes
- watercolour paints
- washable poster paints
- googly eyes
- feathers
- pipe cleaners
- felt fabric squares
- popsicle sticks
- cotton balls and colourful pompom balls
- recyclables such as egg cartons and toilet paper rolls
- white polymer clay to form, bake and paint
- playdough

# Playdough Recipe

1 cup flour

¼ or ½ cup salt (¼ cup salt makes a softer playdough for younger hands)

2 Tbsp. cream of tartar

1 cup water

2 tsp. food colouring

1 Tbsp. oil

Combine the ingredients together in a medium size sauce pan. Cook over medium heat 3 to 5 minutes, stirring constantly until playdough forms a ball in the pan. Knead the dough on a floured surface until it's not sticky and let the fun begin!

Playdough lasts 3 to 4 weeks kept in a sealed plastic container in the fridge.

# Simple Craft Ideas

Ask the question: What did you *see* outside that was happy it was raining? Supply paper and crayons, felt pens or paint.

Gather simple craft ingredients during your walk. Rocks, branches, leaves, cones and even dirt can help your child nourish their creative mind. Let them pick supplies from the craft box and watch the fun begin.

Rocks can be painted or turned into critters by adding googly eyes and ears cut from felt.

Leaf rubbings can be created by placing leaves between sheets of white paper and running a wax crayon gently over them to create an outline. Leaves and branches can also be glued onto paper as the beginning of a picture.

Cones turn into fun friends by adding feathers and googly eyes. Help from an adult with a glue gun would make this easier.

Playdough is a wonderful medium for creating whatever the imagination can conjure up. Part of the fun is in helping make the playdough and picking the colour. The simplest playdough creation; worms, love the rain!

For young children, celebrate rain with warm sudsy water in a sturdy tub placed on a plastic sheet on the ground. Add plastic containers or funnels to the water for a wonderful wet experience.

Painting a piece of paper with poster paint and then setting it outside for a short time to catch raindrops, creates a painting made by your child and nature.

Glue cotton balls to construction paper for clouds or snow and create a picture around them.

Have an adult carve the shape of a raindrop in the top of a potato and create a potato stamp. Dip the stamp in poster paint and then stamp it on paper. This makes wonderful homemade wrapping paper.

Place the stems of white daisies in water with a few drops of food colouring to demonstrate how nature drinks. After 2 days you will begin to see the colour in the white petals.

Type the words 'crafts with egg cartons', or 'crafts with pipecleaners', or any other ingredient in your craft box into an internet search engine and become inspired by all the exciting possibilities!

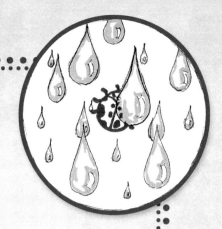

# Author's Biography

Kathy Johnson lives near Victoria on Vancouver Island. When her daughters were young, a walk was always a favourite part of their daily routine. They especially loved those rainy west coast days when you can feel and hear nature's perfect harmony.

Kate Peer lives in Vancouver, where rain is called liquid sunshine. She grew up on a steady diet of wet hiking trips, which gave her a love of nature and a belief that mud completes childhood. An Honours Art student, she hopes this book will be the first of many.